Prayers

AND

Po-Boys

*A Cancer Survivor's Journey
Through Chemotherapy and Beyond*

LARRY SINGLETON

www.mascotbooks.com

Prayers and Po-Boys: A Cancer Survivor's Journey Through
Chemotherapy and Beyond

For more information, please contact:
Mascot Books
620 Herndon Parkway, Suite 320
Herndon, VA 20170
info@mascotbooks.com

Library of Congress Control Number: 2020916715

CPSIA Code: PRV0321A
ISBN-13: 978-1-64307-437-5

Printed in the United States

Dedication

I want to dedicate this book to everyone who has had to bear the burden of being diagnosed with cancer. That is undoubtedly some of the worst news that you could ever receive, and it is truly a life-altering experience. Throughout my ordeal with cancer, there were countless people whose advice, experiences, insights, and perspectives inspired me along the way. *Prayers and Po-Boys* is the story of my journey, and hopefully some aspect of it will do the same for you. Through the proper care and the necessary funding for research, I truly believe that one day we can eradicate this terrible disease. This is becoming a more realistic goal thanks to the work of organizations like the V Foundation, the Stuart Scott Memorial Fund, the MD Anderson Cancer Center, and St. Jude Children's Research Hospital.

Stuart Scott was quoted as saying, "When you die, it does not mean that you lose to cancer. You beat cancer by how you live, why you live and the manner in which you live." In accordance with that, I had dreams prior to my diagnosis, and I still do. For those of you who have larger-than-life dreams, and now in addition to trying to accomplish the impossible, you have the added burden of a cancer diagnosis, my advice to you is simple. Keep dreaming and keep believing! No matter what, always remember that there is no way to measure the power of God or the resiliency of the human spirit. I also want to dedicate this book to all the unbelievable people who are caregivers, who are the support systems—please know that what you do is beyond measure. Always know that every gesture, every sacrifice, and definitely every prayer, those things are everything. God bless all of you!

I can't close this out without giving a shout-out to my support system. I don't want to get into naming names because everything that everybody did meant the world to me, at a time when all of it was needed. For everyone who went above and beyond the call of duty, and did anything that helped me along my path, please know that you played a critical part in today even being possible, and I'll always love you for that! In addition to the daily perils that cancer patients and survivors face, on January 20, 2020, we experienced the first confirmed case of COVID-19 in the United States.

My prayers go out to the people that I've lost and everyone who has lost someone to the pandemic. Lastly, as patients and survivors, we are at an elevated risk of contracting the coronavirus. So, it is imperative that we all remain vigilant, continue to wear masks, and continue to practice social distancing. God bless and be safe!

Lastly, before I begin, I want to take this opportunity to pay homage to Chadwick Boseman, who, on August 29, 2020, lost a four-year battle to colon cancer. Whether he was playing James Brown, Jackie Robinson, or Thurgood Marshall, Chadwick Boseman brought iconic African-American figures to life—though no role of his was more iconic than King T'Challa. His portrayal of the Black Panther marked the first time a black superhero graced the silver screen, thus shattering that proverbial glass ceiling. Chadwick Boseman's legacy is that of a man who used his platform to influence change and to bring awareness to social and racial injustices at one of the most critical junctures in our nation's history. Although his biggest role was that of a fictional character, Chadwick Boseman was a real-life hero, and he will be dearly missed. Wakanda forever!

Chapter One

Despite the fact that December 17 began like any other typical Thursday, the events of that day would forever change my life. My job was physically strenuous, and for months I had attributed my fatigue and weight loss to work-related stress and sleep deprivation. Over time, the combination of the two became too much to bear, and on Thursday, December 17, 2016, I finally made an appointment. After arriving at the University Medical Center, my wife and I were led to an office to meet the attending physician. In the course of telling him what my symptoms were, the doctor noticed an enlarged lymph node just above my collar bone. I'll never forget what he said next. "Larry, I don't want to jump the gun, but based on the swollen lymph node, night sweats, and your drastic weight loss, my preliminary assessment would be that you have a classic case of Hodgkin lymphoma."

The doctor's prognosis didn't register initially. Cancer? That was something you only read about. That was something that happened to other people. I was ordered to remain overnight, and a biopsy would be conducted to determine if the lymph node was in fact cancerous and if it had metastasized. Early the next morning, my wife and I met Dr. Sobia Ozair, who would become my primary physician. Having never had a surgery before, I had a million questions ranging from how anesthesia would be administered, to what the treatment regimen would be if, in fact, the diagnosis was what I feared it would be. When our conversation ended, I was taken to the OR where the biopsy was to be performed. I said a short prayer and closed my eyes before the procedure was done.

On December 22, my worst fears were confirmed. I was told that I had stage four Hodgkin lymphoma and that the disease had already spread to three organs. The days following the diagnosis were filled with uncertainty and retrospection. I thought about everything that I'd planned to do, and faced the realistic possibility of not having the chance to do any of it. I thought about my children and all of the things that I'd intended for them. I thought about how my son was on his way to the Navy, and my daughter was about to graduate from elementary school. I thought about how my death would impact my family and friends. I thought about the aspirations that I had for *Honor Among Thieves*, a novel that I'd just recently published. I remembered lying in the bed and thinking about how strange it was that being faced with the realistic prospect of dying amplified the significance of everything, and it forced me to come to grips with my own mortality. I remembered thinking that if I made it out of this, how I'd never take anything for granted again. Afterward, I prayed until I fell asleep.

The next three days were surreal, and for obvious reasons, it didn't feel much like Christmas. I can distinctly remember how somber everyone was, and on some level, I felt guilty for having cancer. I felt like I'd robbed everybody of the ability to enjoy what was supposed to be the most joyous day of the year. I tried not to show it, but all I could seem to think about was the fact that this could very possibly be my last Christmas. I thought about all that I'd gone through up to that point, and I thanked God for all that He'd done. I prayed that He'd give me the strength to endure this phase of my journey. For the first time in a long time, I got away from the gifts and all the other things that have come to define Christmas, and I reflected on the true significance of the holiday. The purpose of Christmas was to commemorate the birth of Jesus, and with my renewed sense of appreciation, symbolically, it was a kind of rebirth for me.

The week following Christmas went by relatively quickly, and New Year's was already here! It was as if a different light went off in my head every day, and I really started to realize how much I'd taken for granted. I thought about how many people wouldn't get to experience 2016, and I thought about how reaching 2017 wasn't guaranteed. I knew at that moment, that from then on, my New Year's resolution would be the same every year. I would resolve to never take anything for granted, especially making it to a new year.

My next appointment was scheduled for January 5. We arrived at the hospital to find that the lobby was virtually full. I sat next to a man and his wife. The couple appeared to be in their forties, and I wondered which one of them was here for treatment. The woman was called for registration, and her husband waited for her to return. Despite the fact that his wife was the one receiving chemo, it appeared to be taking more out of him. I looked at his face, and he looked like he'd been crying for days.

"I'm Larry." I extended my hand.

"I'm David," he said, shaking my hand.

"Was that your wife?"

"Yes. She's a fighter. At times, I think that this is harder on me than it is on her. Are you here for chemo?"

"Not yet, but I'll be starting soon."

"She's lost her appetite, and she's starting to lose her hair."

"I'm sorry to hear that."

"Sometimes I feel so helpless. I think about all the times that I could have done things that would have made her happy, and now I don't know if I'll get the chance to."

"I don't know what the two of you have gone through, but keep praying and know that the important thing is that you're here now."

"I try to look at it like that."

Before I could respond, my name was called and upon entering the oncology unit, my wife and I were greeted by Dr. Ozair. She was extremely pleasant and optimistic. We were assured that everything that could be done to achieve remission would be done and that keeping a positive attitude was imperative. We discussed the need to extract bone marrow, and the insertion of a port-a-cath to administer chemotherapy. As someone with a childlike phobia of needles, it was almost incomprehensible that in a week I would have to have a needle inserted into a bone, and that I would have a port surgically placed in my chest that would be the site of several injections to come. Doctor Ozair explained that there were different types of anesthesia, and she informed me that I would be put to sleep for the biopsy.

I was completely oblivious to the types of anesthesia and the differences between the types. Dr. Ozair was patient, and she was extremely thorough in explaining the type of anesthesia that would be administered. I would be put under general anesthesia, which meant that I would receive an anesthetic that would act primarily on the brain and central nervous system to make me unconscious and unaware of what was going on. She told me that it would be administered through my circulatory system by a combination of inhaled gas and injected drugs.

Having never been under anesthesia, I worried about waking up during the procedure. Dr. Ozair assured me that after the initial injection, the effects of the anesthetic would be maintained with inhaled gas and additional drugs through an IV line. Dr. Ozair informed me that a biopsy was simply a sample of tissue taken for further examination. She explained the different types of biopsies, and why a surgical biopsy was selected in my case. It was also discussed that laparoscopic surgery was the best option for me because the tissue is hard to reach. She also mentioned that after the biopsy, my tissue sample would be sent to a pathologist to diagnose my condition.

Dr. Ozair also took the time to explain all the potential side effects of chemo. She said that chemo works by killing the fast-growing cancer cells throughout the body. She said that chemo also reduced the number of white blood cells in the body, and that increased the risk of infection during chemotherapy. She told me that fatigue is one of the common side effects of chemo, so I would probably feel tired a lot over the course of the treatment. She also stressed that headaches, muscle pain, stomach pain, and pain from nerve damage were also common.

The list of side effects was never-ending, and there was still more! There was the potential for mouth sores, diarrhea, bouts of nausea, constipation, the development of possible blood disorders, nervous system effects, possible changes in memory and thinking, hair loss, and appetite loss. The ensuing week was surreal. Despite the fact, that I could vividly remember every detail, it was almost as if it hadn't happened. At times it seemed like I left Dr. Ozair's office on the fifth of January, took a nap, and I was on the operating table on the twelfth.

There were no complications with the bone marrow extraction or the port insertion, and I was scheduled to return on the nineteenth. Everything had been such a blur leading up to that point, that for the first time I was actually able to process all that had happened since my initial visit. In the days leading up to my return visit, I felt the area on my chest where the port had been inserted at least a hundred times a day. Each time had an almost dream-like feel to it. On the morning of the nineteenth, I sat on the bed and tried to wrap my head around the journey that I was about to embark upon, and all the things that could potentially come with it.

In the course of preparing to leave for the appointment, a book on the dresser grabbed my attention. A few weeks prior to the diagnosis, Karen, a friend from work, gave me a copy of T.D. Jakes' *Strength for Every Moment: Inspirational Thoughts to Help You on Your Journey.* Between working and pursuing a career as an author, I simply hadn't had time to read it, but I knew that that was about to change. On my last visit, Dr. Ozair warned me that the application of chemotherapy was a very time-consuming process that could take more than seven hours. I made a mental note to be sure to pack that book along with the other things that had been recommended for chemo. The visit went smoothly, but it didn't do much to put me at ease. We agreed that I would begin therapy on the twenty-second with labs, where blood is taken to monitor blood cell counts, which would be followed by my first infusion on the twenty-fifth.

After we were done, I was instructed to go to the Patient Navigator's office. The Patient Navigator was Ms. Tiffany Broussard, and she explained everything that I was eligible for, the various support groups that I could join, and an assortment of other cancer-related programs designed to ease the transition. Ms. Broussard would end up being an invaluable asset in this fight, and I am eternally indebted to her. When I left her office, I was hopeful, but I dreaded the thought of how bad the ordeal could be, and not to mention that I could end up going through all of that for nothing.

On the morning of the twenty-second, my wife and I arrived at UMC's oncology unit for my first lab. The first person that we encountered was the receptionist, Ms. Helen. This was the first time that we met, but she would become a good friend and a pivotal part of my journey. After I registered, she instructed me to wait in the lobby. From there, I went to meet Ms. Karen and Ms. Flo, who went over the registration process in the oncology department, and like Ms. Helen, they too would prove to be a vital part of my recovery.

The registration process went quickly, and the phlebotomist called me in soon after. She could see that I was nervous, and she assured me that everything would be fine. Now and then, someone would say something so profound that I know I'll never forget it. What she told me was nothing short of an epiphany, and I knew that I would never forget it. She said, "I know exactly what you're going through. I've survived cancer twice. The funny thing is that there are forms of cancer that are self-inflicted, like smoking, or working around certain materials that can cause certain forms of cancer, but that was not the case with me. The two times that I've had cancer, it came as a result of things that were already in my body. Sometimes the accumulation of things that you go through in this life will weaken your immune system to the point where your body is incapable of producing the natural antibodies to ward off antigens."

Her words stuck with me, and I thought about what she said for the rest of the day. In the days leading up to my first infusion on the twenty-fifth of January, everyone found out about the diagnosis. It was during that time that I truly realized the extent to which my condition affected me and those who were close to me. I'll never forget how heartbroken my family and friends were when they got the news. There were people who couldn't be in the same room with me without crying. The outpouring of love and support was overwhelming, and I am eternally indebted to those who endured this ride with me. In the days leading up to my first infusion, I prayed constantly and thought about the plethora of people who I knew were also praying for me. My personal crusade to beat cancer was already more than enough of an incentive to fight, and now I had the additional motivation of knowing that I wasn't carrying that cross alone.

Despite all that had happened up to that point, everything still seemed surreal, and it was hard to process that the twenty-fifth was growing closer and closer. In an attempt to take my mind off the inevitable, I started to read T.D. Jakes' book. The first chapter is titled "I Can Do All Things," and it includes an epigraph from the Bible: "I can do all things through Christ who strengthens me (Phil. 4:13, New King James Version)." With the obstacle that I was facing, the significance of the passage was indisputable. Prior to reading this, I always felt that complacency and contentment were synonymous, but that couldn't be further from the truth. In accordance with the passage, we should not be satisfied with complacency and mediocrity, because to do that would be the equivalent of not fulfilling the call of God in our lives. Contentment is in fact knowing with all certainty that God can fulfill every need.

The twenty-fifth was here, and my anxiety level was through the roof! My wife packed a bag of food, and we left for the hospital. As we entered UMC's parking lot, I prayed and asked God for the strength to get me through the unavoidable. There were a few people in the lobby, and for the most part, it was really quiet. Two of the people in the lobby appeared to be sisters, and their conversation was one that I knew would stick with me forever.

"You can't let this get you down."

"How do you not let dying 'get you down'?"

"I can't imagine what you're going through, and I'm not about to sit here and pretend that I do, but you were the one that stayed strong through all of this. When you got the news, you were consoling us."

"And now the wear and tear of always being there for everybody else has finally caught up with me!"

The raw emotion of the response caused her to be louder than she planned to be, and I know that she regretted what she said as soon as it left her mouth. The other woman sobbed uncontrollably, as the statement cut like a knife. I tried to look at it from both perspectives, and I just kept thinking about how unfair life could be at times. I tried to imagine how differently people viewed life when they knew that death was imminent. I didn't know either of the women, and I didn't know the diagnosis, but I knew that they were at the most critical point in their journey thus far. That conversation reminded me that my journey was just beginning, and that a lifetime of things could happen between the diagnosis and the conclusion. Gradually, everybody left the lobby. By the time I was called, the lobby was empty. Ms. Helen greeted us as we entered the oncology unit, and as always, she was charismatic and upbeat.

"So, today's the big day, huh?" she asked.

"Yeah, this is my first day of chemo."

"It looks like you two are going on a picnic!" She laughed.

"The doctors keep telling me that I probably won't be able to eat anything, so I guess we're about to find out."

"Don't worry, everything is going to be fine," she assured me.

As we talked, I was called to register. Ms. Karen and Ms. Flo were in their normal places in the oncology unit's registry. Like Ms. Helen, they also laughed about the amount of food that I'd brought.

"That's all food?" Ms. Karen asked.

"Yep."

"One of the things that I've noticed is that a lot of people who go through chemo typically complain about nausea and don't eat much."

"I don't know how my body is going to react to chemo, but I certainly plan to eat."

"Well, I wish you all the best and please know that you're in our prayers."

"Thanks, I need it."

"After you get weighed, you can go to the back. Theresa is going to be your chemo nurse, and she's waiting for you."

As we walked through the double doors of the chemo unit, Ms. Theresa and Ms. Patricia greeted me and my wife.

"This is Patricia, and after she takes your vitals, I'll be in to administer chemo," Ms. Theresa said, directing me to room 5.

I was extremely nervous, and my blood pressure was sky-high. Ms. Patricia told me that my blood pressure was so high that I wouldn't be able to receive treatment. I assured her that my elevated blood pressure was a result of me being nervous about my first round of chemo. Over time, my blood pressure lowered to an acceptable level, and it was time. Ms. Theresa warned me that the needle was big, but that the pain from the initial stick would be over quickly. I explained to her that I had an irrational fear of needles, and my heart raced as she walked toward me. The pain was excruciating, and I dreaded the thought of having to have that done in the future. Ms. Theresa explained that she would begin the process with a saline solution through the IV.

She could see that I was nervous, and she carefully explained that the pre-medication drugs had to be administered first, which included steroids for energy and anti-allergy drugs that would probably make me sleepy. She left and returned with small bags of the pre-medication drugs. After the pre-medication drugs had been administered, she told me that the first infusion would be a trial run to ensure that I didn't experience any of the side effects that can accompany chemo, like shortness of breath or an erratic heartbeat. After she connected the bag to my port, I watched intently as the bag's contents went into me. As the bag emptied, I remember thinking, *So far, so good*. Ms. Theresa returned to check to see if I felt any of the symptoms associated with bad reactions to chemo. I told her that I felt fine, and she returned with a larger bag. After she connected the larger bag and left, I proceeded to grab a shrimp po-boy from the bag of food that my wife had prepared. Upon reentering the room, Ms. Theresa couldn't conceal the disbelief on her face.

"I thought that was clothes in the bag! All of that's food?"

"I keep hearing about how everybody on chemo suffers from nausea, and I know that I have to eat, so I'm trying to condition myself to keep my appetite up through this."

"I've been doing this for twenty years, and you are the only person that I've ever seen bring a bag of food to get chemo."

A few hours had passed, and I was exhausted. I was trying to think of something to do to pass the time, and I remembered the book that I'd brought: *Strength for Every Moment*. The message from the first passage held a strong degree of personal significance for me, and the second passage Jakes mentioned was no exception. It read,

> He gives power to the weak, and to those who have no might He increases strength. Even the youths shall faint and be weary, and the young men shall utterly fall, but those who wait on the Lord shall renew their strength; they shall mount up with wings like eagles, they shall run and not be weary, they shall walk and not faint (Isaiah 40:29–31 NKJV).

As I finished the second passage, I heard the door open behind me. I assumed that it was Ms. Theresa returning, and I was surprised to hear a man's voice say, "How are you? I'm the Chaplain here at University. If you don't mind, I'd like to pray with you."

"Absolutely!"

"I see I interrupted your meal," the chaplain said, laughing at what was left of my shrimp po-boy.

"That's okay, I'm going to be here for a while."

"I don't see very many people eat in here."

"I'm trying to be the exception to that rule."

Chaplain Philip Peavy prayed with me, and he assured me that God had plans for me. When you encounter people that have truly been touched by the presence of God, you can tell because they exude the confidence that comes with living a purpose-driven life. I knew that Chaplain Peavy was definitely one of those people. Over the course of my journey, Chaplain Peavy would prove to be an inspiration and a true friend.

When Chaplain Peavy left, I clicked through channels and stopped on ESPN to watch the highlights from the NFL's conference championships. The analysts discussed how the Patriots had made it to the conference championship by beating the Chiefs in the divisional round. The Chief's signature had been stellar defense all year, but the inspirational story of a particular Chief's defender would forever change the way that I viewed discipline and perseverance. The segment was about Kansas City Chief's strong safety, Eric Berry. After complaining about chest pains, Berry was diagnosed with Hodgkin lymphoma on December 8, 2014. He was subsequently placed on the Chief's non-football illness list, which ultimately ended his season. After a grueling chemo regimen, he was cleared to resume football activities on July 28, 2015. I remember staring at the screen in awe thinking about how determined he had to have been to have gone through chemo, and that he was ready to play pro football in less than a year! Not only had he returned to football, but he was selected to the Pro Bowl, was named Comeback Player of the Year, and by many, he was considered to be the best safety in football. Even though I was optimistic, I couldn't help but think about how valiantly Stuart Scott fought before losing his battle with cancer in January of 2015. I remembered his speech, and I could still hear his words clearly:

"So live. Live. Fight like hell. And when you get too tired to fight, lay down and rest and let somebody else fight for you."

The first phase of chemo was complete, and I had finished my first infusion. I felt relieved initially, but that feeling soon gave way to apprehension when I remembered that there was a seemingly endless list of potential side effects. I remember walking out of the chemo unit and seeing people of all ages and nationalities going through the same hell that I was experiencing. I remembered the tears and uncertainty on the faces of the family members in the lobby. My next appointment was scheduled for the second of February, and on the way home, all I could seem to think about was how many people cried thinking about the uncertainty of my situation. I was glad to finally make it home where watching TV might help to take my mind off of the proverbial elephant in the room. I clicked through channels until I got to ESPN. I love football, and I knew that the highlights from the conference championships would allow me a much-needed break from my dismal reality. I'm sure that it just seemed that way because of what I was going through, but it seemed like every other commercial was an advertisement for Neulasta or the Cancer Treatment Centers of America.

I'm sure that I'd seen those commercials a million times before that, but I knew at that moment that I would look at them differently from that day forward. I think that that was the first time that I truly grasped the gravity of my circumstances, and for the first time, I fully understood that I would never look at anything the same ever again. I thought back to what the chaplain said about God's plan for me. A light went on, and I realized that life was all about vantage points. I thought about what I was going through, and all that

I had been through up to that point. I realized that whatever God's plan was for me, my ability to see things from different perspectives and be able to intimately relate to those who were suffering would be a critical part of it.

For the first few hours, everything seemed fine, but that would soon change. My muscles started to ache, and even though I wasn't cold, I was trembling. I remembered hearing the nightmares about all the negative side effects that went with going through chemo. I remembered thinking that if I was experiencing side effects after the first infusion, then that was a sign that my body would not adjust well to chemo. I prayed and braced myself for what I knew would be a grueling process.

Chapter Two

I WOULD SPEND THE DAYS leading up to my next visit getting acclimated to my mandatory pill regimen. There was dexamethasone, which was the steroid, and ondansetron (Zofran), for nausea. I knew that I had a long way to go, but up to that point, I hadn't suffered any of the side effects that typically accompany chemo. I attributed my newfound appetite to the steroids. At the time of the diagnosis, I was 166 pounds, and when I was weighed on the day of my first infusion, I was 185 pounds. I'm probably the biggest advocate for Melba's Old School Po-Boys and Gene's Po-Boys on the planet! From a physical standpoint, my ability to eat proved to be invaluable in my recovery. Being from New Orleans, I had been accustomed to eating good food all my life, and until now, I realized how much I'd taken that for granted. I was so afraid of being nauseous, and not being able to eat, that I overate to try to condition my body to be able to consume food during chemo. As the days passed, with everything else that I was experiencing, I thanked God that eating hadn't been a problem. My appetite was insatiable, and with nausea being common throughout chemotherapy, everyone was surprised with my capacity to hold food.

The second of February came, and I was looking forward to telling Dr. Ozair that I hadn't experienced any side effects. She said that I looked like I was handling chemo well. Deep down I know that I was relieved to hear that, but all I could remember was that I had low sodium levels, low blood potassium, and too much of this and not enough of that. She reminded me that my next lab was scheduled for the nineteenth. I remember laughing to myself, thinking, *So, my next impalement is in about two weeks*. I knew that there were a lot of things that I was supposed to start doing, but the only things that seemed to stick were that I needed to eat more fruits and vegetables and increase my water intake.

A week had passed since my second doctor's visit, and the city was vibrant with Mardi Gras euphoria. Mardi Gras was always a special time, but this year in particular, it seemed like everyone was enthralled with Fat Tuesday bliss. I had two reasons to celebrate that day, as February 9 is also my daughter's birthday. Mardi Gras was something else that I'd grown to take for granted, and I hadn't been to a parade in years. Now I wanted so badly to go to a parade, but I couldn't because of the risk of infection. With that realization, I vowed that if it was in the Lord's will that I lived to see the next Mardi Gras, I wouldn't miss a parade!

In the days leading up to labs, my body had adjusted well, and I had continued to gain weight. When we arrived at the hospital, I was surprised to see that I had a different phlebotomist. I thought back to the conversation that I'd had with the first one about how the things that we go through in this life can contribute to various forms of cancer, and how strange it was that she was there to tell me that at the beginning of my journey. Ironically, I never saw her again. It was as if God had put her there specifically to deliver that message on that day. I left and tried not to think about the upcoming infusion. I just kept eating and praying.

The morning of my next treatment came way too fast, and I remember standing in the shower, dreading the inevitable. I remember standing in the mirror rubbing lidocaine (Emla), an anesthetic cream for numbing the skin during medical procedures, around the area where my port was located. I can remember smiling, listening to my wife pack the food that she'd prepared. As we pulled out of our driveway, I realized that I'd never asked what she'd cooked. She started to respond, but before she could answer, I saw the po-boys in the bag.

The registration process was becoming familiar, and I almost looked forward to the staff laughing about all the food that I'd brought. Like clockwork, Ms. Helen was the first person that we saw. Ms. Helen has a natural charisma and a magnetic personality that I'm certain every patient she ever encountered is thankful for.

"Good morning!"

"Good morning, Ms. Helen."

"What's on the menu for today?" she asked, pointing to the bag I was carrying.

"Shrimp po-boys, fully dressed."

"It looks like you've gained weight."

"About twenty pounds."

"Keep praying! Everything is going to be fine. They're going to call you in a minute."

I took a seat in the lobby, and I remember how exhausted everybody looked. The toll that cancer took on its victims and their support systems was undeniable. I grabbed a copy of

Time, and I flipped through its pages trying to find anything to read to take my mind off of the hours to come. I was reading an article about Bono, the lead singer of U2, and how his philanthropic acts were changing the world, when someone walked up and sat next to me.

"Is this seat taken?" a woman asked, pointing to the seat next to me.

"No, not at all."

"I'm Susan. Are you here for chemo too?" She extended her hand.

"Yeah, it's my second infusion. I'm Larry." I reached to shake her hand.

"It's my fourth. Have you had any side effects?"

"Yeah, but so far nothing too serious."

"You're lucky because I can't eat at all."

"So far, I've been okay with that."

Before she had a chance to respond, I was being called to register.

"It was nice meeting you Susan, and I hope that everything goes well," I said, as I stood up.

"Thank you, and I hope that everything goes well with you too."

I walked through the lobby and down the hall to the registry.

"How are you today, Mr. Singleton?" Ms. Flo asked.

"All things considered, I'm good. The other lady isn't here today?"

"No, Karen's off today."

"Both of you were here, but I remember that she registered me last time."

"No food today?"

"Yeah, it's in the lobby."

"What's on the menu today?"

"Shrimp po-boys."

"You don't look like you're going through chemo, what's the secret?"

"Prayers and po-boys! You gotta pray, and you gotta eat!"

She laughed and told me that they were waiting for me in the back.

As we entered the chemo unit, I could see that Ms. Patricia was seated at the first desk, and I could see that she was laughing as we got closer.

"Lasagna? Gumbo? Jambalaya?"

"No, po-boys."

"What kind?"

"Shrimp."

"Dressed?"

"Of course!"

She directed us to room 5, and she said that she'd be back to take my vitals. As usual, my blood pressure was sky-high, and again, I had to wait for my pressure to stabilize so that chemo could be administered. In the course of waiting, I was startled by a bell ringing and what sounded like a celebration afterward. I couldn't wait for Ms. Patricia to return to ask her what had happened. Before I had a chance to ask, she walked into the room and was already talking about "the bell."

"I know you're looking forward to that!"

"Looking forward to what?"

"They ring the bell whenever someone completes chemo."

"Then I'm definitely looking forward to that!"

Ms. Patricia proceeded to take my pressure, and it was the lowest that it had been since the process started. We laughed about how maybe it was the discussion about the bell that brought my pressure down. Ms. Theresa entered the room, and even though we didn't take my pressure again, I'm certain that it was as high as it was the first time it was taken. I said a silent prayer and prepared myself for the second infusion. The needle still hurt, but the Emla reduced the pain tremendously. I sat back and got as comfortable as the circumstances would allow me to, and I turned the TV on. I went to ESPN to watch the sports highlights from the previous day, just as the chaplain entered.

"How are we today?"

"Blessed."

"Yes, you are my friend! I'm surprised you're not eating!"

"I'm about to. I was just getting situated when you walked in."

"What's for lunch?"

"Shrimp po-boys."

"From where?"

"These are homemade."

"Smells great!"

"They are."

"When you get a chance, you have to go to Jacque-Imo's and try the roasted duck and alligator cheesecake!"

"I started to turn down the alligator cheesecake, but if I make it through this, alligator cheesecake it is!"

We laughed, prayed, and talked about the Cleveland-Oklahoma game, and LeBron's chances of winning the championship. It was always uplifting to talk to the chaplain, and that day was no exception. The chaplain had to make rounds throughout the entire hospital, and he apologized for having to leave so soon. I assured him that I knew that he was doing God's work and that I appreciated the time that he was able to stay. As the chaplain left, I looked at the amount of fluid left in the bag and knew that I had about four or five hours left. I spent the remaining time eating my po-boys and reading. So far, my journey had been filled with epiphanies, and the third passage quoted in *Strength for Every Moment* didn't disappoint:

> And at the end of the time I, Nebuchadnezzar, lifted my eyes to Heaven, and my understanding returned to me; and I blessed the Most High and praised and honored Him who lives forever . . . At the same time my reason returned to me, and for the glory of my kingdom, my honor and splendor returned to me. My counselors and nobles restored to me, I was restored to my kingdom, and excellent majesty was added to me. Now I, Nebuchadnezzar, praise and extol and honor the King of Heaven, all whose works are truth, and His ways justice. And those who walk in pride He is able to put down (Daniel 4:34, 36–37 NKJV).

Contrition is the key. Asking for help when you've fallen is essential, not only from a spiritual standpoint but in everyday life as well. The remaining time went quickly, and before I knew it, it was time to leave.

Chapter Three

About an hour or so after I got home, I felt completely different. Up to that point, there had been few side effects, but I knew that that was about to change. If you're fortunate enough to never have to bear the weight of cancer, then I can imagine that it would be difficult to understand pain on a cellular level. For lack of a better explanation, everything hurt. My mind raced, and I prayed that this was not a foreshadowing. I had two relatives that died as a direct result of refusing to take chemo. At the time, I couldn't understand why they'd stopped receiving chemo when they knew that the consequences would be dire and final. I knew that I wouldn't give up, but I also understood why they did. I understood at that moment that I wasn't afraid of dying, but I was deathly afraid of the thought of not living first.

The intensity of the pain subsided, but it returned periodically for the next few weeks. For the most part, I was able to stay optimistic, but the grim reality was that the castle walls had been breached and the barbarians were at the gate. Fear wasn't a common emotion for me, and this was unchartered territory. I looked back at every obstacle that I'd had to over-come, and I realized that the difference was that no matter what I was going through at the time, there was always a foreseeable end, a light at the end of the tunnel. With cancer, on the other hand, every aspect of your life changes with the diagnosis. Whether it's the way you feel, the discomfort of the port, or whether it's the inability to do things that at one time were second nature, you have to come to grips with the fact that you've experienced a chemical change. Even beyond the obvious physical wear and tear, there is the mental anguish of trying to cope with the never-ending, looming uncertainty.

When you hear stories about peoples' bouts with cancer, it's understandable that it's easy to get preoccupied with the enormity of the illness. Through my own experience, and through talking to other people who had taken the same journey, I realized that the physical battle was a very small part of it. It's everything else. All of the same headaches that were there prior to the diagnosis aren't just there anymore, but now they're amplified. Creditors couldn't care less about the weight of your cross, and the first of the month always seems to come way too fast. Cancer doesn't make provisions for dream chasers. Whatever time constraints existed before were now intensified.

The times between infusions were getting shorter and shorter, and it was already time for another one. The date was March 3, 2016, and my third injection was scheduled for the next day. I found that television and the internet usually took me to a place where cancer wasn't at the center of my every thought, and I found asylum in both. In an attempt to take my mind off of my impending treatment, I clicked through channels until I ran across a news story about Rod-ney King. I remembered it like it happened yesterday, and it was hard to believe that twenty-five years had elapsed since that dreaded day in 1991. For the first time in a long time, I didn't think about my circumstances at all. I thought about Trayvon Martin and Mike Brown. I thought about all the political unrest in the world, and how unstable and volatile things really were. With all the things in this life that were prone to change, I took that opportunity to thank God for the things in my life that were stable.

Finally, the seventh was here, and it was time to start what had become my chemo day ritual. The food was packed, the Emla had been applied, *Strength for Every Moment* was in the side compartment of the bag that contained my food, and last, but definitely not least, I prayed. We left for the hospital, and for the first time, Ms. Helen wasn't there when we arrived. I realized at that moment how much I had grown accustomed to seeing her, and how much she influenced my ability to keep a positive outlook. I had developed a routine, and my "team" was a critical part of that routine. It had become an essential part of my regimen that I see her as soon as I walked in the door. In my personal war, she was the first line of defense. I walked down the hall to the registry, and I was relieved to see that Ms. Karen and Ms. Flo were there. The rest of my "team" was there.

"How are you today, Mr. Singleton?"

"No complaints. Where's Ms. Helen?"

"Helen's on vacation; she'll be back Friday."

"I was getting worried; I'm trying to keep the same team that I started this journey with."

"Don't worry about that, we're going to be here. Well, you look great."

"Thank you."

"Po-boys today?"

"No, it's spaghetti."

The registration process went quickly, and I proceeded to the chemo unit. Normally, I didn't see Dr. Ozair unless I had an appointment to see her, so I was surprised to see that she was sitting at one of the desks. As I turned the corner, I could see that she was talking to a patient. I walked up to greet her, but before I could speak, I was interrupted by the bell. The three of us smiled, as we knew that the ringing of the bell symbolized someone completing chemo.

"How are you, Larry?"

"I'm good, Doc. Just waiting on my turn to ring the bell."

"I remember when they rang it for me," the patient who was standing at the desk said.

"I'm Larry." I extended my hand.

"I'm John, you look like you're handling chemo well."

"I have a chest scan coming up, and let's hope that it says the same."

"It was great meeting you, and please know that you'll be in my prayers, Larry."

"Thank you, and congrats on finishing chemo!"

The look on Dr. Ozair's face and the awkward silence that followed said everything.

"I finished chemo, but I'm not in remission. There's nothing else they can do."

"I'm sorry."

"I fought the good fight, and I'm at peace."

We said our farewells, and I proceeded to room 5 as usual. Ms. Patricia and Ms. Theresa came in shortly after. With the experience that I'd just had, it was a major relief to know that the rest of my team was there.

"Po-boys?" Ms. Patricia asked. She fastened my blood pressure cuff.

"No, it's spaghetti today."

"From where?"

"It's homemade."

"You cooked today? No po-boys?" Ms. Patricia asked my wife.

"Other than po-boys, most of what I eat is homemade."

"Is her cooking better than Melba's and Gene's?"

"Absolutely."

"How could your pressure always be this high?" Ms. Patricia looked at the blood pressure gauge.

"I think it's knowing what happens next."

"I forgot you don't like needles."

My blood pressure eventually went down, and Ms. Theresa came in for the injection. In contrast to the previous times, this particular infusion was uncharacteristically less painful. The chemo unit was unusually packed that day, and Ms. Theresa had to hurry off to administer another infusion. I got settled and managed to finish my spaghetti before Chaplain Peavy made his rounds. When he came in, he was upbeat and full of charisma, and I looked forward to seeing him.

"How are you guys today?" the chaplain asked my wife and me.

"We're good, Chaplain, and you?"

"I'm fine. I'm surprised you're not eating," the chaplain said, through a chuckle.

"I finished before you got here."

"Let me guess, po-boys?"

The chaplain and I talked about everything from sports and politics, to the best places to eat in the city. The chaplain and I prayed before Ms. Theresa came in to change the bag.

"I hate to go, but I still have a lot of people to see."

"Thanks for everything, Chaplain, and we'll see you next time."

"Take care, Larry, and keep praying!"

The bag's contents drained quickly, and before I knew it, it was time to go. As always, the process was draining, and I was looking forward to lying down. The twenty-four hours following chemo were always the most exhausting part of the process. Usually, I was able to rest the next day, but I was scheduled to see Dr. Ozair to discuss how I was handling chemo up to that point. The only thing that seemed note-worthy was that I'd started to notice a slight discoloration in my cuticles.

We arrived at the hospital early the next morning, and Dr. Ozair was already waiting with two other physicians. Each of them complimented me on not looking like I was going through chemo. That meant a lot whenever anybody said it, but it seemed to carry a little more weight when it came from a doctor. Dr. Ozair told me that I still had a long way to go, but my lab work showed that the tests that preceded chemo all showed significant improvement. Though I still had to increase my potassium levels. I told her about the discoloration of my nails, and she assured me that there was nothing to worry about. The condition was called *melanonychia*, and it was commonly associated with strong chemo regimens. She gave me a list of signs that would let me know if it was developing into a more serious condition. So far, everything had gone relatively well, and that played a crucial part in my overall outlook.

Chapter Four

In the weeks leading up to my next lab, I continued to gain weight, but gradually I started to feel bouts of fatigue. I began working on a manuscript for a zombie novel, titled *Ground Zero*. I'd known people who'd gone through chemo, but for the first time, I truly understood how draining the process was and why it was so draining. Chemo kills dividing cells, so it also affects healthy tissue where cells are constantly growing and dividing. The skin, bone marrow, hair follicles, and the lining of the digestive system are examples of cells that are constantly growing and dividing. Over time, the process of chemo killing various cells became too draining, and it was too hard to focus on writing. Needless to say, I put *Ground Zero* on the backburner and focused my attention strictly on recovery. I promised myself that if I survived chemo, I would definitely finish writing that story.

In past weeks, parking had become a problem, and the hospital started to issue parking decals for patients in the oncology unit. Other than that, the visit was relatively monotonous. The labs visit was uneventful, and the next three days went quickly. It seemed like the times between infusions were getting shorter, and it was hard to believe that it was already time again.

"What do you want to eat tomorrow?" my wife asked.

"Lately, I've been craving meatloaf and mashed potatoes."

"Gotcha."

The next morning, we got up and started the ritual early. We double-checked everything and headed to the hospital. As we arrived, we saw all the parking tickets that had been issued to cars without the parking decals on their windshields. We parked and made sure that the parking pass was clearly visible before we entered UMC's cancer unit. The lobby was about half full, and the vibe was very somber. We proceeded to where Ms. Helen was seated.

"How are we today?" Ms. Helen asked from behind her desk.

"No complaints."

"What's in the bag?"

"Mashed potatoes and meatloaf."

"No po-boys?"

"I go off the reservation sometimes, but I always come back."

Our conversation was interrupted by my being called to register. Ms. Karen and Ms. Flo were in their normal places, and as always, it was good to see them.

"How are you today?" Ms. Flo asked.

"Blessed and highly favored."

"That's what I'm talking about!"

"Is this labs, or is this a chemo day?" Ms. Karen asked.

"Chemo."

"Keep praying, and know that we're praying for you too!"

"Thank you, I will."

"After you get weighed, Theresa is waiting for you."

After I got weighed, my wife and I walked through the double doors of the chemo unit. Ms. Patricia was the first person that we saw.

"Good morning!"

"Good morning, Ms. Patricia."

"Room 5 is open. I'll be in there in a second."

"Okay."

For the first time, my pressure was low enough to administer chemo without needing a second reading. Moments later, Ms. Theresa entered the room with the chemotherapy drugs.

"Good morning!"

"Good morning, Ms. Theresa."

"I was watching something about Golden State, and how they're trying to catch Michael Jordan's record. You think they can do it?"

"It's going to be hard to catch 72–10, but if there was a team that could do it, it would be them."

"You a fan?"

"I'm a Lakers fan, but I'm also a fan of history and a fan of greatness. I wish the Golden State all the best, and I hope they pull it off. I think it would be good for the sport."

"What do you think about Hillary winning Missouri?"

"I was watching something about that last night, and I think that win pretty much gave her the democratic nomination."

"Do you want her to win?"

"Definitely. That goes back to the Golden State thing: obviously, she's qualified and I think she'd be a great president, but the historic significance is immeasurable. If she were to win, that would be two historic presidential terms in a row. Think about what that would do for future generations. The proverbial glass ceiling would be shattered forever. There would be no such thing as an unrealistic goal.

"That's a good point. Well, you ready to get this over with?" Ms. Theresa put on a pair of rubber gloves.

"I'm never ready for this."

Thankfully, the injection was quick, and for some reason, I was a lot more relaxed than I had been for prior infusions. Usually, I'd start reading or clicking through channels, but this time, I just sat back and enjoyed my thoughts. I remembered the 95–96 season when the Bulls went 72–10, and how I thought that that record would never be broken. I thought about how Golden State had a very realistic chance of breaking that record. I thought about Hillary Clinton possibly being the first woman president.

We were in the midst of a changing of the guard, and you could feel the tension and the optimism. I smiled when I thought about that, and then, at that moment it occurred to me that the reality of it was that I might not be there to witness either outcome. I realized that no matter how optimistic you are, cancer has a funny way of reminding you of your mortality. I spent the remainder of the time reading and reflecting on everything that had led up to that moment.

The weeks leading up to my next hemogram, or complete blood count, were routine, but that day would end up being a defining moment in my journey. As usual, we arrived at the hospital early, and there was only one other person in the waiting area. After I registered, I sat a few seats down from the woman, who was still in the lobby awaiting treatment. She had on a black and gold scarf, which was usually an indication that the Adriamycin in chemo had caused her to lose her hair. Her name was Judith, and she was there for chemotherapy as well.

"Good morning," she said, in a somber tone.

"Good morning."

"I'm Judith." She extended her hand.

"It's nice to meet you, Judith. I'm Larry." I reached out to shake her hand.

"Are you from here?"

"Yes, are you?"

"I'm originally from here, but I moved to Slidell after Katrina."

"You miss living in the city?"

"There's no place like home, but I have family there, so it's cool. How far along are you?

"Monday is my fifth infusion."

"I have labs today, but next week I begin my second month of chemo."

"How has it been for you?"

"In the days following my first infusion, I completely lost my appetite. It's like my taste buds just stopped working, and I lost the desire to eat. When I finally reached a point where I felt like I could eat something, I started to develop sores in my mouth, which made eating pretty much impossible.

"I'm sorry to hear that. The Zofran doesn't help?"

"It did in the early goings, but that was short-lived. How has it been for you?"

"So far, I've been fortunate as far as eating. Chemo is such a draining process that I can't imagine trying to deal with this and not being able to eat. My heart truly goes out to you."

"Thank you. If you don't mind me asking, how did you find out?"

"I started experiencing night sweats, and I was tired all the time. I came in to get a checkup and was told that I had stage four Hodgkin lymphoma. And you?"

"About a month or so before I came in, I started to notice that my breasts had become overly sensitive to the touch. I feared that I had some form of cancer, but I don't have any family history of cancer, so I felt optimistic. The doctors felt a small lump, and after a 3D mammogram, they were just about certain what it was. The blood work came back, and I was diagnosed with stage three invasive ductal carcinoma."

In the course of talking to Judith, I realized that despite the severity of my diagnosis, things could have been far worse. I was called to see the phlebotomist, and Judith and I wished each other well. By the time I was finished, Judith had left. Until that day, labs had always gone quickly, and I usually was never there long enough to hold a conversation. It was as if God had placed her there to deliver that message.

I thought about all the people that had been passers-by in the oncology unit, and I thought about how each of them represented a different journey. We were all connected by a common adversary, but every story was different. No two diagnoses were the same, and no two stories were the same. The only details that remained consistent were that cancer ravaged entirely too many people and took an extensive toll on way too many families.

I never saw Judith again, but if by some chance she reads this, I want her to know that she is still in my prayers, and I hope all is well.

Chapter Five

The day of my fifth infusion was here, and I was still thinking about my conversation with Judith. I could tell that she was optimistic and that she wanted to live, but the wear and tear of the combination of cancer and chemo was undeniable. I thought about everything that we talked about, but for some reason, Judith's inability to eat kept reverberating in my head. I thought about what I wanted to eat that day, and even though I'd already made eating a priority, I think that was the first time that I truly understood how blessed I was just to be able to eat at all. I smiled when I thought about how important po-boys had become in my regimen, and I smiled again when we made a stop at Melba's. As we arrived, I was surprised to find that there was only one person in the lobby again. I'd lost track of how many times I'd been to the hospital since my diagnosis, but I was certain that those were the only two times that had ever happened. The man in the lobby appeared to be in his late fifties, maybe early sixties, and he appeared to be in good health. Usually, I could tell the difference between people who were there for treatment, and the people that were there to support them, but this time I couldn't.

"Good morning." He looked up from his magazine as he greeted me.

"Good morning."

"Are you here for chemo?"

"Unfortunately."

"Me too. This is my first one."

"This'll be my fifth."

"You don't look like it! How much do you weigh?"

"I'm about 210, but I was 160 when this started."

"They keep telling me that I should prepare myself for nausea, and possibly not being able to eat. What's the secret?"

"I know that every situation is different, but I find that a big part of not having an appetite comes from worrying about trying to beat cancer. My advice in those situations is to remember that it's not cancer that you're beating, the key is to focus on surviving chemo. Trust God and trust the process. Have faith that the treatment regimen will work and make eating a focal point. Chemo destroys the cancer cells, but it damages healthy cells as well, so if you don't eat, chemo will eat you."

"I never looked at it like that, and that makes a lot of sense. I apologize, I'm Travis." He stood and extended his hand.

"I'm Larry." I stood and shook his hand.

"What type do you have?"

"Hodgkin lymphoma."

"What stage?"

"Four."

"I have stage three hepatocellular carcinoma."

"How did they detect it?"

"I had been feeling fatigued for a few months, but I just thought that it was because I'd started working more hours. About a month or so ago, I started having fevers and losing weight, and I knew that something was wrong. When the blood work and all of the scans came back, they showed that I had cancer. After he went through my records, the doctor saw that I had a history of Hepatitis B, and that's what they think caused my cancer. The type that I have is the most common type, and it's treatable, but the bad thing is that it usually goes undetected until it's in the later stages."

"Hopefully, you adjust well to chemo."

"I've prayed over it, and I know that God will see me through this. No matter what the diagnosis is, they can't measure your desire to live."

"Touché."

It was always inspiring to see people with such vigor for life, despite facing such dismal circumstances. Our conversation was interrupted by the nurse letting me know that I was next to be registered. By the time I returned from registration, Travis had already gone to the back to begin his stint with chemotherapy. My mind went back to Judith, and how our conversation had helped me. I hoped that my conversation with Travis would prove helpful throughout his travels. I picked up the magazine that he was reading, an issue of *Time* from June 13, 2016.

The page that was facing up contained an article written by Jillion Potter, a rugby player who'd survived cancer. In the article, she said that she was in Paris, playing in the World Cup, and three weeks later she was diagnosed with stage three synovial sarcoma. I knew all too well what Jillion meant when she said that even with all the love and support, cancer takes a toll on your body and your heart that she wouldn't wish on anyone.

The entire article was powerful, but there was a particular excerpt that really stuck with me. This is what it said:

> But here is what they don't tell you about cancer: Life still happens—the good parts too—even when you're sick. You still get to make memories and laugh until you cry and try new things. It may be different than before, and the shadow of cancer may be lurking behind you, but magically life still happens. And you appreciate it even more post-diagnosis.

My thoughts went back to Judith, and how at various points in your life, God sends messengers. Just as I was finishing the article, the nurse came out to tell me that they were ready for me in the chemo unit. As usual, Ms. Patricia was the first person that I saw.

"Well, good morning, Mr. Singleton!"

"Good morning, Ms. Patricia."

"What's for lunch?"

"You already know!"

We laughed and proceeded to go to room 5. Ms. Patricia fastened my blood pressure cuff and placed the thermometer under my tongue. She looked at the monitor, and we both laughed as she shook her head.

"I'll be back to take your pressure again in a few minutes," Ms. Patricia said before she left the room.

Ms. Theresa came in shortly after. Her smile told me that Ms. Patricia had already told her about my blood pressure.

Over the course of the next few minutes, my pressure dropped to a level where it was safe to receive chemo. As many shots as I'd received up to that point, somehow, I just never seemed to get used to needles. I gritted my teeth as the needle pierced the first layer of skin, and then again, when the pressure was applied to ensure that the needle had gone deep enough into the port. I ended up being there for six hours, but the time seemed to fly. Before I knew it, the infusion was over, and it was time to leave. As always, chemo was exhausting, and I couldn't wait to rest. I had five infusions under my belt, and I was looking forward to the end of this grueling process.

We returned home to find that I had a letter from my son. He'd successfully completed basic training in the Navy, and he'd be home in a few months. With all that was going on, that was some much-needed good news. That was one of the proudest moments in my life. I feel like the brave men and women that serve in our armed forces are true heroes that make the ultimate sacrifice every day.

To know that my son was now a part of that elite fraternity meant more than words could ever express. It felt good to let him know that my recovery was going well and that we all missed him dearly. I couldn't wait to see him in his uniform! I thought about the infinite number of times that my children have made me proud, and it was almost as if I could hear Stuart Scott's 2014 ESPY speech all over again. "The best thing I've ever done, the best thing I will ever do is be a dad to Taelor and Sydni. I can't ever give up because I can't leave my daughters. I love you girls more than I will ever be able to express. You are my heartbeat . . . The most important thing I do is I'm a dad." I know exactly what he meant.

The next day I thought about the conversation that I'd had with Travis and the letter that I'd written to my son. For the first time, it dawned on me how much I'd learned about cancer over the months that had passed. We talked about the various stages of cancer, symptoms, the difficulty in detecting certain forms of cancer, and the list goes on. In retrospect, my vocabulary was now filled with terms that I probably would have otherwise never had a reason to use. Words like *phlebotomist, oncologist, remission, relapse,* and *carcinoma* had become a natural part of my vernacular. In those times, I realized just how much cancer affected every facet of your life.

When you begin chemo, there is a recommended regimen that is based heavily on your diagnosis and other biological factors. With the high risk for infection and the countless other things that could go wrong, treatments could change depending on the circumstances. I'd seen so many cases of people who were initially recommended for chemotherapy, and ended up completing chemo, and then being forced to endure radiation therapy. If all went well, I was more than half-way through chemotherapy, and now it would all come down to the chest and pelvic scan, which would be in a few months. No matter how much weight I'd gained, or how many side effects I'd been blessed to avoid, everything was contingent on my CT scan.

Chapter Six

I spent the weeks before my next infusion thinking about all the things that I'd wanted to do prior to the diagnosis. I thought about all the people who had fought courageously, and they still ended up succumbing to cancer. I thought about all the plans that they had, all the people that they loved, and all the things that they would've done differently if they'd known how their story was going to end. I vowed that if it were in the Lord's will that I survive this, I would never take anything else for granted ever again. I always felt like my life was purpose-driven, but now I had a renewed sense of determination.

I tried not to dwell on my upcoming CT scan, and I did a lot of reading and watched a lot of TV to try to take my mind off it. I was lying down, clicking through channels, and the guide showed that *America's Got Talent* was about to come on. It registered to me that *America's Got Talent* had been on for several seasons, and I'd never seen one episode. I was intrigued, and I looked forward to seeing exactly what the show was about. Up to this point, there had been numerous times where I knew that God had put me in a particular place to go through a specific experience. I had no idea that one of the most significant moments of my life would come as a result of watching a reality talent contest. I hadn't laughed that hard in a long time, and Julia Scotti, a transgender comedian, was just what the doctor ordered! Aside from just admiring her courage, Julia was genuinely funny.

Calysta Bevier was next, and after receiving my life-altering diagnosis, it felt good to be blindsided in an inspirational way. Calysta is a sixteen-year-old singer who was diagnosed with dysgerminoma, which is a form of ovarian cancer. Following the removal of a five-pound tumor, multiple chemo infusions, and numerous hospital stays, Calysta is now in remission, and she is a powerful advocate for cancer awareness. (It never ceases to amaze me just how many lives this terrible disease had affected.)

Before she sang, Calysta told the crowd, "I came here today to show people that, no matter what you've gone through, to keep chasing your dreams." I knew that statement would stay with me forever. Calysta performed a rendition of Rachel Platten's "Fight Song," and there was not a dry eye in the house. Over the years, Simon Cowell has proven to be a brutal and unrelenting judge, and even he was compelled to use his Golden Buzzer to send Calysta straight to the quarterfinals. I'd heard that song before, but now it held a completely different significance. I still can't get that song out of my head!

Chapter Seven

I didn't realize how time had crept up since my last hemogram, and it was already time for my next one. Even though I tried not to think about it, every trip to the hospital brought me closer to my dreaded CT scan. Obviously, I wanted to know the results, but I had to find a balance somewhere between optimism and bracing myself for the worst. After meeting Judith and Travis, I fully expected to meet someone in the oncology unit's lobby, but to no avail; no one was there. The lobby was completely empty. As always, it was comforting to see that Ms. Helen was there.

"Well, good morning, Singletons!"

"Good morning, Ms. Helen," my wife and I said, in unison.

"You here for labs or chemo?"

"Labs."

"This has been a slow day; you should be in and out."

Other than people already receiving chemo, the oncology unit was virtually a ghost town. Ms. Helen left to make sure that I could register. She returned quickly, and that was usually a telltale sign that the registry was vacant. My wife waited in the lobby while I registered.

"Good morning, Larry."

"Good morning, Ms. Flo."

"Labs, right?"

"Yep."

Ms. Karen walked up just as I responded.

"How are you today, Larry?"

"I'm good, Ms. Karen, and you?"

"I'm fine, thank you."

"After you sign your consent form, you can go straight in."

"Thank you."

"You okay? You don't seem like yourself today?"

"I'm worried about the CT scan coming up."

"You're going to be fine. Trust that God hasn't brought you this far for nothing."

Ms. Flo's words stuck with me long after my hemogram, and long after I'd left the hospital. Despite the countless changes that I'd experienced throughout this ordeal, my faith in God was unwavering. I learned early on that from one day to the next, you had no idea how you were going to feel, or what part of your body would hurt that day. Every day was a fight, and for the first time I understood why infusions were called "rounds." Cancer's signature was uncertainty, but the presence of God brought certainty and stability. God's grace had brought me this far, and I knew that it would bring me through.

I hadn't read *Strength for Every Moment* in a while, and now seemed like an ideal time to start back. The last passage that I'd read was "Day 29," and the bookmark was still on page 185. The passage was fittingly titled "Run with Endurance." Each passage begins with a Bible passage, and this one was dead on: "Therefore we also, since we are surrounded by so great a cloud of witnesses, let us lay aside every weight, and the sin which so easily ensnares us, and let us run with endurance the race that is set before us" (Hebrews 12:1 NKJV). No matter what obstacles are set before us, the key is to trust in God and continue to run the race. This is true, not only in terms of battling cancer, but in every area of life.

The day that I'd grown to hate was here. It was time for my next infusion. Despite how important eating had become throughout this process, this was the first time that I didn't want anything specific to eat. The lingering effects of chemo were starting to catch up with me, and getting ready was considerably harder than it had been before. It seemed like the smallest tasks took everything. I prayed for the strength just to get through the day. It felt like it took forever, but eventually, we made it to UMC. Ironically, the lobby was full, in contrast to the past few visits. In addition to how the day was already flowing, to my dismay, Ms. Helen wasn't there either. We took a seat in the lobby and waited to be called for registration. I remember looking around at all the people there, and even though each of us had a different story, we were all there as a result of the same affliction. Even the children in the lobby were somber. It was as if they all could grasp the gravity of the situation.

There were people in wheelchairs, people with portable oxygen tanks, and a sea of blue, emesis nausea bags. Through it all, I realized that I still had so much to be grateful for. About ten minutes had passed, and I was called to register. As I walked toward the registry, I passed two women who were standing in the hallway crying. The younger of the two women was consoling the other one. She told her that she had to be strong and that her diagnosis wasn't necessarily the end of the story. Having only heard that part of their conversation, I knew all too well what they were talking about. Bad news and tears were commonplace in the oncology unit. One way or the other, everyone there had received news that would forever change their lives. Registration went quickly, and I just wanted to get the day over with. I entered the chemo unit, and as usual, Ms. Patricia was there to greet me.

"Good morning, Mr. Singleton! No food today?"

"I wasn't really hungry. I'll probably get something from the cafeteria later."

"Your suite awaits," Ms. Patricia said, pointing to room five.

I took a seat and waited for her to return to take my vitals. Before she returned, the bell sounded. The sound of the bell ringing was a pleasant change of pace from the pain and misery that typically defined being in the chemo unit. It was always reassuring to know that someone was finished with this chapter of their life. I can't explain how I knew, but I just knew that my time was coming. Ms. Theresa came in to give me the injection, but I was so preoccupied with the conversation that I'd heard, that I barely felt the needle. Ms. Theresa left the room, and Chaplain Peavy walked in right behind her.

"How are you today, Larry?" The chaplain extended his hand.

"I'm good," I said. I reached for his hand while being careful to not disconnect the IV.

"I'm surprised you're not eating!"

"I'm sure that I'll eat before I leave, but I don't really have much of an appetite right now."

"You know that I'd love to stay, but I still have a lot of rounds to make. I'd like to pray with you before I leave."

"Absolutely."

We prayed and, as always, the chaplain's words left me feeling enlightened and hopeful.

"Larry, it's always a pleasure, keep praying!"

"Chaplain, please know that what you do here is equally as important as what the doctors do, and I truly appreciate it."

"Thank you, that means a lot."

"No, Chaplain, thank you!"

The chaplain left and I remembered thinking about the number of scheduled infusions that I had left before my bell was rung. The remaining time passed, and before I knew it, Ms. Theresa was disconnecting the catheter. The infusion was done, and I was glad to be finished. I had gotten in the habit of leaving my phone in the car during infusions, and when I made it to the car, I was surprised to see that I had so many missed calls and messages. Each missed call represented someone who was concerned about me, and even though no call or message was any more important than any other, one stuck out. It was from a childhood friend that I hadn't talked to in years. The message read, "I tried to find you on social media, but I couldn't find you. I got your number from your mom. Please CALL ME! You are in my prayers, and please let me know if you need ANYTHING!!!!!!" I called him as soon as I got home, and it was just like old times. He told me that he'd talked to a few people that had seen me since I'd been receiving chemo, and they mentioned that I didn't look like I'd been through that. I told him that I appreciated it, but there was so much more to chemo than physical appearance.

I didn't want to go on a rant about how debilitating chemotherapy is, but I wanted him to understand that despite how I looked, I was far from okay. He told me that when we got off the phone, he was going to send me something that he wanted me to read. By the time we got off the phone, I'd forgotten what he said, and when I got a text message alert, I was surprised to see that it was from him. It was a link to a video. The video was a six-second vine clip of a man missing a half-court shot at a college basketball game. I laughed when I saw it, just as I had every time that I'd ever seen anybody miss similar shots.

The story that followed the video ended up being an emotional one, and equally as inspirational. It was the story of Scott Park. Scott Park was an environmental engineer for the Navy, and he'd been battling life-threatening illnesses for the past eight years. Park won an all-expense-paid trip to the ACC tournament, and he was subsequently given a chance to shoot a shot from half-court to win a million dollars. Park took the shot, and it came up short. The video ended up going viral. As the video went on, Park said that he could remember a point where five organs were beginning to shut down simultaneously. With a failing kidney, liver, spleen, gallbladder, and pancreas, doctors were baffled, and they had trouble even coming up with a diagnosis. Over time, they concluded that Park had a rare blood disorder called Catastrophic Antiphospholipid Syndrome (CAPS). The disease is so rare that at that time only 400 cases had ever been diagnosed.

Despite two years of dialysis treatments, his kidneys never responded. After he received a transplant from a church member, miraculously, Park was the only person with CAPS to have ever received a successful transplant. In hindsight, Park had to overcome very serious medical issues just to have the strength to walk out onto the court, much less being able to make a half-court shot. Scott Park showed true courage, and I'll never forget that story. I knew after I watched the video that my friend wasn't comparing my situation to the adversity that Scott Park was facing, but showing me that he understood that physical appearance isn't always accurate in terms of judging a person's well-being.

Chapter Eight

The time leading up to my next hemogram was a blur, and before I knew it, it was time for labs again. Whether it was labs or an infusion, I hated anything to do with needles, but I grew to appreciate the fact that labs took considerably less time than chemo, which made it the lesser of the two evils. As we arrived at the hospital, it was a major relief to see that Ms. Helen was back.

"How are we today?"

"It's good to see that you're back!"

"I was a little under the weather, but I'm much better now."

"That's good to know. It's probably this crazy weather."

"I think that's exactly what it was. Today is labs, right?"

"Yep."

"You can have a seat in the lobby. I'll call you when they're ready for you."

"Okay."

My name was called, and I proceeded to go to the registry. I walked up to find that Ms. Karen and Ms. Flo were talking.

"Good morning!"

"Good morning, Larry. How are you today?"

"I'm good. How are you two?"

"We're good," they responded, almost in perfect unison.

"That's good."

I registered and waited to see the phlebotomist. I never had the same one twice, and today would be no exception. She was extremely good at drawing blood, and by the time I had braced myself for the needle, she was done. I said my farewells to my team and left. On the ride home, all I could think about was my upcoming infusion and the all-important CT scan that followed.

I stayed upbeat and optimistic in the days following labs, but knowing that the CT scan would be about a week later, it grew difficult to hide the anxiety. The moment of truth was right around the corner. I'd always had a great relationship with God, and with what I was facing, I knew that I needed Him more than ever. There are times in everyone's life that will test the stamina of their faith, and this was certainly one of those times. I smiled when I realized that I'd been so fixated on my CT scan that I forgot that after the scan, I had one more infusion before my bell was rung! The magnitude of the scan had been weighing so heavily on me that I lost focus of the fact that I was almost finished with chemo! As grueling as the process had been, it still was brief in contrast to what some others have been forced to endure.

Even in the face of such dismal circumstances, there still was so much to be thankful for. God had pulled me out of the fire so many times already that I had a renewed confidence that even this potentially fatal weapon would not succeed against me.

The days passed, and I continued to pray and eat. It was the day of my last infusion before the scan, and I felt a strange type of calm, which was especially odd for a chemo day. As usual, we got up early that morning and started, what had become, the chemo ritual. I took a long shower, applied the Emla, and allowed enough time for it to take effect. Sticking to the regimen, my wife packed an assortment of food, and we left for the hospital. When we arrived, I smiled as we entered the empty lobby. It was like Judith and Travis were there. I walked through the lobby to Ms. Helen's desk, and as always, she was in her normal, charismatic mood.

"Good morning, Singletons!"

"Good morning, Ms. Helen," my wife and I said.

"Don't you have a CT scan coming up?"

"It's in a little over a week."

"You nervous?"

"A little."

"Don't be, just keep praying!"

"Always."

"Know that you're in our prayers!"

"Thank you, Ms. Helen."

"You can go and register."

"Okay."

Ms. Karen was typing when I walked up, and I noticed that Ms. Flo wasn't at her desk.

"How are you?"

"I'm fine, Ms. Karen. Is Ms. Flo off today?"

"No. She should be right back. You're almost done!"

"Yeah, I have a CT scan after this and one more infusion."

"You handled it well. God has truly been with you on your journey."

"Absolutely!"

"You can go straight to the back."

"Thank you, Ms. Karen."

"You're welcome, Larry, and take care! We're praying for you!"

I walked toward the chemo unit, and I could see Ms. Patricia through the double doors at the entrance.

"Well, how are we this morning?"

"I'm good, Ms. Patricia."

"I guess we can get ready to take your pressure three or four times."

"Maybe more," I replied. We both laughed.

"You're in 5."

"Next time I come, it'll be for the CT scan."

"Just keep praying, you'll be fine, and you know that we're all praying for you!"

"Thank you!"

It was strange that as many times as I'd been stuck throughout my treatments, the thought of needles still had that effect on me. As expected, my pressure was too high and had to be taken again. After multiple attempts, my blood pressure finally reached a level where chemo could be administered. Ms. Patricia left to attend to another patient, and Ms. Theresa came in soon after.

"How are you doing?"

"I'm good, Ms. Theresa. How are you?"

"I'm fine. Don't you have a scan coming up?"

"It's in about a week."

"Everybody's praying for you!"

"Thank you, Ms. Theresa."

"You have one infusion left after this! It's almost time for you to get your bell!"

"As bad as I want that, at times it's hard to believe that that time is here."

"You've come a long way."

"I couldn't have done it without all of you."

"Awww!"

"Seriously, I mean that."

Ms. Theresa checked to ensure that my port allowed a good blood return and started the infusion. She checked to make sure that the chemo drugs were flowing smoothly through the IV and left the room. I reclined in my chair and thought about all that had transpired up to that point. The rooms in the chemo unit were positioned along the streetcar route, and I loved to watch them pass. The view was picturesque, and it was a perfect way to pass the time. I must have been really lost in whatever I was daydreaming about because I didn't notice that Chaplain Peavy had walked into the room.

"Am I interrupting anything?"

"No, not at all."

"How's everything?"

"I'm good. I have a CT scan in about a week, and that's going to tell the story."

"Well, let's pray."

"I'm glad you came because I definitely wanted to pray with you before the scan."

The chaplain prayed and talked with me for a while before he had to continue his rounds. Ms. Theresa came in periodically to check on me, and before I knew it, the infusion was over. She disconnected the catheter, and I had made it through another session with no complications. I thanked God for having brought me that far, and then we headed toward the parking lot.

Chapter Nine

The day of my long-awaited CT and pelvic scan was finally here. Despite how I felt, everything rested on the results of those tests. I hadn't slept a wink, and I knew that I would be on pins and needles until the results came back. As we pulled up to the hospital, I remember replaying everything that had happened up to that point. There were moments where it all seemed surreal, and at times, I had to feel the area where the port was put in my chest to remind me that this was very real. As opposed to registering in the oncology unit, I was instructed to go to a different part of the hospital. I had a CT scan done with the initial diagnosis, but I hadn't been in any other part of the hospital since.

The radiology department was on the second floor, and it seemed like the elevator took forever. When I reached the second floor, I checked in and was handed a large bottle of an oral contrast. The oral contrast was a liquid that contained barium. Barium is a chemical element, with a chalky taste and texture, that allows doctors to see the lining of your organs. The nurse instructed me to drink the contrast and to not eat anything, as the liquid took sixty to ninety minutes to distribute fully into the bowels. It was only a little over an hour, but the time that the liquid took to fully distribute, felt like an eternity.

The time finally passed, and I was led to the room where the CT scanner was located. The radiologist Instructed me to lie on the procedure table, where he inserted an IV to allow contrast dye to flow through my veins. The CT scanner was a large cylinder, with an X-ray source in the inner ring that rotates around you, and it emits beams of X-rays which are detected by the X-ray detectors. At various points throughout the scan, you're required to hold your breath as the scanners produce images of whatever part of the body is being scanned. The scan was over quickly, but it was the most nerve-wracking ten minutes of my life! To add insult to injury, I had to wait five days for the results, in addition to having another hemogram and an infusion in the same time frame. God had pulled me through countless situations, and I knew that this too would come to pass.

I knew that as a precautionary measure, I would have to have blood work done long after I was done with chemo. Even though I knew that this wouldn't be my last infusion, it was significant because it could possibly be my last one prior to the CT scan. If the results of the scan showed that I was in remission, I would have one infusion left! It had been a hard-fought battle, and I was looking forward to my bell. My thoughts were a collage, and I thought back about how much had happened since my diagnosis. I thought about how I hadn't even known Dr. Ozair for a whole year, and in a few days, she'd deliver what would be, arguably, the most important news of my life.

My thoughts were erratic, but I stuck to the stability of the regimen that had gotten me that far: I continued to pray and eat. The days leading up to my last infusion went well, and I was relieved that the day was finally here. As usual, we got up early and headed to the hospital. I don't know why the memories of that day are so vivid, but I can remember clearly how pretty the weather was. I can even remember the guard putting tickets on the windshields of cars without the parking decal. We walked through the lobby and saw Ms. Helen talking to a woman at the desk. As we got closer, I could hear that the woman was upset about the results of her hemogram. She was saying something about a discrepancy with her platelets. She was frantic, and Ms. Helen was trying to console her. Even though we'd never met, my heart went out to her, and I could only imagine what she and her family were going through. I gave her and Ms. Helen time to finish talking before I walked up to the desk.

"Good morning, Ms. Helen."

"Good morning, Larry. How are you?"

"I'm good."

"That's good! Keep praying and keep thanking God! I just spoke with a lady, and she's not handling chemo well. It's a major blessing that you've handled chemo as well as you have."

"Yes, it is, and I never take it for granted."

"This is a lab day for you, right?"

"Yep. When I come back in three days, that might be my last infusion."

"Keep praying! You'll be fine."

"Thank you."

"You can take a seat in the lobby."

After a few minutes, Ms. Flo came out to let me know that I was next for registration.

"Good morning, Ms. Flo."

"Good morning, Larry. You're in 3," she said, pointing to the third booth in the registry.

"How have you been?"

"I've been okay. How about you?"

"I'm okay, looking forward to my last infusion."

"They're about to ring your bell! That's a blessing!"

"Yes, it is!"

"After you sign this, you can go straight to the back."

"Thank you."

Labs went quickly, and as we left, all that I could think about was the bell. I prayed a lot during the next three days, as the weight of the scan started to bear down on me. I had faith that everything would be fine, but the grim reality was that the results were uncertain, and my life hung in the balance. The last time that I saw Dr. Ozair, I had shown tremendous improvement and things were going as scheduled. Those things gave me a reason to be optimistic, but they were in no way a guarantee. The day of the infusion had arrived, and I was up way earlier than usual. I wanted to get an early start, and I began the ritual a few hours earlier than I normally did. I didn't have an appetite, and I told my wife not to pack anything. I knew that if I got hungry later, I could always get something from the hospital's cafeteria. When we arrived, Ms. Helen was there to greet us, as usual.

"Good morning! Today's the big day, huh?"

"Good morning, Ms. Helen, and yes, it is!"

"Congratulations! You've come a really long way!"

"Thank you, and it has definitely been a long journey!"

"You can have a seat. They'll call you in a minute."

"Thank you."

I took a seat in the lobby and started to flip through a copy of *New Orleans* magazine. I didn't realize that I'd sat directly next to somebody, and his words startled me.

"Are you here for treatment?"

"Yes."

"I'm sorry. I'm Kevin." He extended his hand.

"I'm Larry. Are you here for chemo?"

"No. I'm here with my mom. She just started."

"Is she getting chemo now?"

"No. I'm just waiting on her to register."

"I wish her all the best. This is my last infusion."

"I look at what my mom goes through, and I know you're glad that this is over."

"You couldn't imagine."

"Larry Singleton," the nurse yelled from the registry.

"It was nice meeting you, and I wish you and your mom the best," I said as I got up.

"Thank you, and congrats on finishing."

"Thanks."

I passed a lady in the hallway leading to the registry, and I just knew that she was Kevin's mom. I could tell that she'd been having a hard time with chemo. There is a specific type of exhaustion that accompanies chemo, and I knew that she was all too familiar with it. I waived at Ms. Flo as I walked to the vacant booth in front of Ms. Karen's desk.

"Good morning, Ms. Karen," I said as I walked past her desk.

"Good morning, Larry! This is the last one, right?"

"Yeah."

"Congratulations! You're getting your bell today!"

"I can't stop thinking about it."

I took a seat and waited for Ms. Karen to finish typing.

"Good morning, Mr. Singleton. How are you?"

"I'm doing great! Today is the last one!"

"Congratulations!"

"Thank you!"

"They're going to ring the bell for you today!"

"I can't wait!"

"They'll call you in a minute."

"Okay."

By the time I got back to the lobby, Kevin and his mother were gone. I was sure that I would see them in the chemo unit. I hoped that hearing my bell would inspire Kevin's mother like it inspired me when I heard it. A few minutes passed, and I was called to the chemo unit. As usual, Ms. Patricia was the first person that I saw.

"Good morning, Mr. Singleton."

"Good morning, Ms. Patricia. How are you?"

"I'm fine, and you?"

"I'm ready to get it over with."

"I almost forgot! Today is your last one!"

"Yep. I get my bell today!"

"You earned it."

We continued to talk as we walked to room 5. I sat down while Ms. Patricia left to get a blood pressure cuff.

"This is your last one, so we should only have to do this once, right?" Ms. Patricia asked me when she re-entered the room.

"I doubt it."

Ms. Theresa walked in while we were laughing about my blood pressure being high again.

"This is your last one! Your pressure should be perfect!"

"Good morning, Ms. Theresa."

"Good morning, Mr. Singleton! How are you?"

"I'm good, just ready to get it over with."

"You get your bell today!"

"I can't wait."

Eventually, my pressure came down, and it was time to administer my last infusion. Ms. Theresa inserted the needle and checked my blood return. The return was good, and she hooked the first bag to the catheter. It felt good to know that this was the last time that I'd be here for hours.

About an hour or so passed, and Chaplain Peavy came into the room.

"How are you, Larry?"

"I'm okay. How are you?"

"I'm fine."

"This is my last infusion."

"Congratulations!"

"Thank you. It's been a long time coming!"

"Praise God."

"Absolutely."

The chaplain and I talked for a while, and we prayed before he left. I looked back at the bag to see how much was left. I knew that it was the anxiety, but it seemed like the bag was still full, and almost two hours had passed. I watched *Sports Center* to pass the remainder of the time. I dozed off, and I was awoken by Ms. Theresa telling me that I was done. After she detached the catheter, I was startled by the bell ringing. Without warning, the staff of the chemo unit came in to congratulate me, and to give me my bell. I had played this moment in my head a million times, and it didn't seem real. I fought back tears thinking about all that I'd been through to get to that point. I thanked everyone and then just paused to savor the moment. Ms. Theresa handed me my bell, and for a moment in time, nothing else mattered.

We laughed and talked for a while, before everyone eventually left the room. I stared at my bell for what felt like an eternity. I thought about everyone who had the chance to experience that, and my heart went out to the ones who didn't. Throughout my journey, I'd seen both ends of the spectrum, and I knew how blessed I was. As I walked out of the chemo unit, I waived to Kevin and his mother. I could read her lips through the glass, and she said, "Congratulations."

I whispered back, "Thank you."

Chapter Ten

The morning came quickly, and the day of reckoning was here. I'd played out every possible scenario in my mind, and now I was going to get the results from my CT scan. I expected to be nervous, but surprisingly I wasn't at all. It was about 9:45 a.m., and the appointment was for 10:30. We got to the hospital around 10:15, and I remember not being able to find a parking spot. I remember laughing to myself and thinking, *Of all days for this to happen.* We eventually found a parking spot, and I could feel the tension rising as I got closer to hearing the news. The walk from the parking garage seemed longer than usual, but I attributed that to the whirlwind of thoughts that were swirling through my head. In no time, we'd made it to the oncology unit, and I was one step closer to the conclusion. There were a few people in the lobby, and Ms. Helen was at her desk.

"Good morning! Today's the big day, huh?"

"Good morning, and yes, today is the day."

"You should be excited!"

"I'm a little nervous."

"Don't be! You've done everything that you could, now leave the rest to God!"

"You're right."

"They'll call you in a minute to register."

"Okay."

I waited in the lobby, and I prayed silently until I registered. A few minutes passed, and I heard my name called. Every time that I'd registered before felt pretty much the same, but because of the nature of the visit, this time felt very different. As I approached her desk, Ms. Flo could see that I was anxious.

"Today's the big day!"

I nodded.

"What's wrong?"

"Nothing's wrong, I'm just a little nervous."

"That's understandable, but God has brought you this far, and you have to trust that He will continue!"

"I know that this is one of those times where there is only one set of prints in the sand, and more importantly, I know why. I have 100 percent trust in God, but I think it's only human nature to worry sometimes. I think that's a big part of why we lean on Him so much."

"I understand, Larry, but you're going to be fine."

"Thank you, Ms. Flo."

"You're welcome, and as soon as you get the good news, make sure that you stop by and tell us."

"You know this will be the first stop I make, no matter what the news is."

"Keep praying and know that we're praying for you too!"

"Good luck, Larry," Ms. Karen said, returning to her desk.

"Thank you, Ms. Karen."

"You're going to be fine! Keep praying!"

I nodded and walked back to the lobby. I took a seat and continued to pray. I thought that I would have more time in the lobby, but the nurse called me mid-prayer.

"Larry Singleton, Dr. Ozair is ready for you."

The walk to Dr. Ozair's office seemed like the longest walk in the world! When we finally made it there, I was surprised to see that she wasn't there.

"You can have a seat, Dr. Ozair will be in to see you in a minute."

I sat down and my mind raced, as my doctor's absence increased the angst. After what seemed like an eternity, Dr. Ozair came into her office, and the first thing that I noticed was that she had a very big smile on her face. I smiled and let out a sigh of relief, since I couldn't fathom that she'd be smiling while she was coming to deliver bad news.

"Good morning, Larry! How are you?"

"Well, Doc, I guess that depends on what you're about to tell me."

"Well, Larry, I'm happy to tell you that you are in complete remission."

Before I responded, I closed my eyes and allowed the news to sink in. Once what she'd said had fully registered, I thanked God and hugged Dr. Ozair.

"Dr. Ozair, thank you for everything!"

"You're very welcome, Larry. You were still scheduled for a few infusions, so as a precautionary measure, we'll still go through with those. After that, it'll be all port flushes."

I thanked Dr. Ozair again, and as I walked out into the hall, I bumped into Ms. Tiffany.

"How are you, Larry?"

"I'm in remission!"

"Congratulations!"

"Thank you!"

I normally didn't see Ms. Patricia or Ms. Theresa unless it was a chemo day, but I had to share the news with them. When I made it to the chemo unit, I was glad to see that they were at the desk together.

"Good morning." I greeted her as I walked up to where they were seated.

Ms. Theresa looked up from her monitor and said, "Good Morning! You don't have chemo today, do you?"

"No. I came to tell you and Ms. Patricia that I'm in remission!"

"Congratulations!" they both said, as they got up to hug me.

"Did you tell Ms. Helen?" Ms. Patricia asked.

"Not yet, but you know I wouldn't leave without telling her."

We talked for a minute before I left to tell everybody else. I was glad that my whole team was there to share that moment. Ms. Helen was at her desk, and she asked about the results before I had a chance to tell her.

"So, how'd it go?"

"I'm in remission!"

"Thank God!"

Ms. Helen got up from her desk to hug and congratulate me. We talked for a while, and then I went to share the news with Ms. Karen and Ms. Flo. When I went to the registry, I was glad to see that they both were still at their desks.

"Guess who's in remission?" I said, making my way to their desks.

"Congratulations!" they said, practically at the same time.

"Thank you."

"I can't imagine how you must feel!"

"I don't think that there are any words that could describe this!"

I was on cloud nine for the rest of the day, and I remember that I couldn't stop smiling. I knew that I still had to go through chemo a few more times, but with the news that I'd just received, that didn't bother me at all. I prayed and thanked God for carrying me through that process, as He'd done so many times before. I sat on the edge of the bed, and I stared at my bell. I thought about the significance of what that bell really meant. I knew that my bell symbolized the fact that God's grace had saved me again, and I knew that from that moment forward, I would always keep that bell close to me.

Chapter Eleven

Not long after my doctor's visit, my wife told me that her grandmother wanted to talk to me, and that it was very urgent. I knew that whatever she wanted to tell me was important. Her grandmother had been battling cancer on and off for over three decades, and doctors finally concluded that all options had been exhausted and her condition was terminal. We went over later that day, and we were surprised to find that her grandmother was up watching *Jeopardy!* When we entered the room, I could tell that she was happy to see me.

"Larry, how are you? I've been praying for you!"

I had so much that I wanted to say, but her words rendered me speechless. I found it amazing that with what she was facing, she was still concerned with my well-being. I'll never forget her, and I'll never forget the conversation that we had.

"Larry, I want you to listen very carefully because I don't have much time."

"I'm listening."

"I want you to stick to what the doctors tell you to do and keep fighting!"

"I will. I promise."

I knew that that was her way of saying that despite the fact that she'd reached the end of her journey, there was still time for me. Words would never be able to express what that conversation meant to me. I showed her my bell and told her that I was in remission. We talked for a while longer, and then I left to allow her time to rest. I had a chance to see her one more time after that. She passed away the following week. I remember attending her funeral and thinking about what she said. I thought about how precious and how short life really is. I said a silent prayer for her as I rang my bell. I speak for everyone who knew her when I say that she is loved and dearly missed.

In the weeks following her funeral, I remember being home one day while T.D. Jakes' talk show was on. The subject of that particular show was turning pain to power. The guests on the show were all people who had experienced catastrophes in their lives, and they had found ways to channel their adversity into positive things that allowed them to move on. One of the guests was a woman who'd used archery to channel all the negative feelings from what she'd experienced. T.D. Jakes explained to her that it was ironic that she chose archery as a form of therapy, since the same principles that governed archery worked the same in life as well. He explained that much like the force that it takes to propel an arrow forward, oftentimes, the things that have played such a critical part in holding you back, will ultimately provide the same power that it takes to propel you forward. I thought about how exhausting my experience had been, and how invigorated I felt now.

I thought about how optimistic my outlook had become. Cancer had definitely played a big part in limiting the things that I could do, and now I felt like the possibilities were endless. The bishop's logic weighed heavily on me, and I've been thinking about his words ever since. Even though I'd never met T.D. Jakes, that didn't change the fact that his insight had played a pivotal role in not only, my physical recovery, but my personal growth as well.

On November 29, I had a port flush scheduled. This time was different, even though I'd had this procedure done before. My birthday is on November 30, and when this journey began, there was no guarantee that I would see this one. My team played as big a part in my recovery as anything had, and I wanted to show my appreciation by bringing them autographed copies of my novel, *Honor Among Thieves*. When I arrived at UMC, I handed out the copies in the order that I saw my team members. Ms. Flo ended up being last.

"Good morning, Larry."

"Good morning, Ms. Flo."

"How are you?"

"I feel great! Tomorrow is my birthday!"

"Well, happy birthday! What's this?" Ms. Flo asked when I handed her the book.

"That's my book, *Honor Among Thieves*."

"Thank you! And you signed it!"

"Of course."

"You have a powerful story to tell, and you're a writer! That's your voice! You have to write about this! Your advice could help someone else on their journey! What would you tell somebody else who was going through what you went through?"

"Keep praying and keep believing, and last, but definitely not least, keep eating! Prayers and po-boys will save your life!"

"That's a catchy title, and that's what you should call it! Prayers and Po-Boys!"

The conversation with Ms. Flo stuck with me, and I made my mind up in that moment that I was definitely going to write about my journey. After I registered, I walked into the chemo unit and for the first time, I didn't see Ms. Patricia or Ms. Theresa. As usual, I walked into room 5 and watched TV until they got there. The first thing that I saw was a news special commemorating the end of hurricane season. I thought about how ironic it was that my birthday marked the end of hurricane season, and it was an opportunity to celebrate the end of my personal storm as well. I turned the channel and went to ESPN to see the highlights from the Packers and the Eagles' Monday night game. I never did get to see the highlights, but what I did see just added another epiphany to the countless number of life-altering experiences that I'd already gone through since my diagnosis.

The segment that was on was a piece commemorating the tenth anniversary of V Week for Cancer Research. That was the second major thing in a row that was taking place on my birthday. Jim Valvano announced the commencement of the V Foundation in March of 1993, while he accepted the Arthur Ashe Courage and Humanitarian Award. While delivering his speech, Valvano announced that the foundation's motto would be "Don't Give Up . . . Don't Ever Give Up." Valvano was diagnosed with adenocarcinoma, which is a type of bone cancer, in June of 1992. Valvano died less than two months after delivering what would become one of the most inspirational speeches of all time.

I thought back to what Ms. Flo asked me regarding my advice to those who were forced to bear the burden of this terrible disease. I'd been thinking about that non-stop since she posed the question. I couldn't come up with anything, and when the segment concluded, I realized that one of Jim Valvano's signature quotes from that 1993 speech summed it up perfectly. "Cancer can take away all of my physical abilities. It cannot touch my mind, it cannot touch my heart, and it cannot touch my soul. And those three things are going to carry on forever. I thank you and God bless you all."

To Judith and Travis, I don't know how things are going with you, but wherever you are in your individual journeys, please know that I'll never forget you, and you're not alone!

Author Bio

L arry Singleton is a life-long Louisianian, author, and screenwriter. He is also a cancer survivor. In December of 2015, Larry received the dreaded news that far too many people have, or have yet to, receive: he had stage four Hodgkin lymphoma, and it had spread to three organs. Having already lost relatives and friends to this terrible disease, Larry knew all too well that his diagnosis could prove to be terminal, despite the substantial strides made in cancer treatments in recent years. Through a steady diet of po-boys, prayer, and undying faith, Larry beat the odds and is currently in remission.